W9-ARB-280

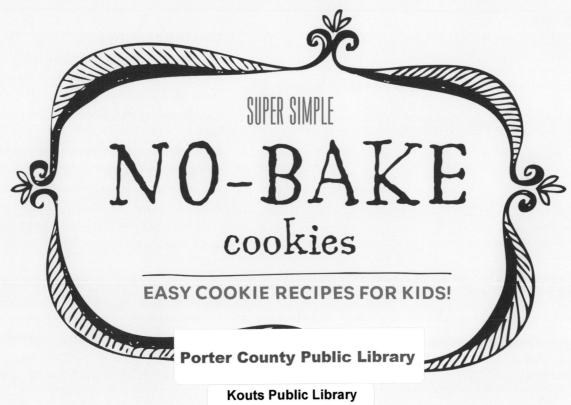

SUPER SIMPLE

NO-BAKE

cookies

EASY COOKIE RECIPES FOR KIDS!

ALEX KUSKOWSKI

Consulting Editor, Diane Craig, M.A./Reading Specialist

abdopublishing.com

Published by Abdo Publishing, a division of ABDO, PO Box 398166, Minneapolis, Minnesota 55439. Copyright © 2016 by Abdo Consulting Group, Inc. International copyrights reserved in all countries. No part of this book may be reproduced in any form without written permission from the publisher. Super SandCastle™ is a trademark and logo of Abdo Publishing.

Printed in the United States of America, North Mankato, Minnesota
102015
012016

Editor: Liz Salzmann
Content Developer: Nancy Tuminelly
Cover and Interior Design and Production: Mighty Media, Inc.
Photo Credits: Mighty Media, Inc., Shutterstock

The following manufacturers/names appearing in this book are trademarks: Brer Rabbit®, C&H®, Karo®, Market Pantry™, Oreo®, PAM®, Philadelphia®

Library of Congress Cataloging-in-Publication Data

Kuskowski, Alex, author.
  Super simple no-bake cookies : easy cookie recipes for kids! / Alex Kuskowski.
    pages cm. -- (Super simple cookies)
  ISBN 978-1-62403-950-8
1. Cookies--Juvenile literature. 2. Desserts--Juvenile literature. 3. Cooking--Juvenile literature. I. Title.
  TX772.K778 2016
  641.86'54--dc23
                    2015020617

Super SandCastle™ books are created by a team of professional educators, reading specialists, and content developers around five essential components—phonemic awareness, phonics, vocabulary, text comprehension, and fluency—to assist young readers as they develop reading skills and strategies and increase their general knowledge. All books are written, reviewed, and leveled for guided reading and early reading intervention programs for use in shared, guided, and independent reading and writing activities to support a balanced approach to literacy instruction.

TO ADULT HELPERS

Help your child learn to cook! Cooking lets children practice math and science. It teaches kids about responsibility and boosts their confidence. Plus they get to make some great food!

Before getting started, set ground rules for using the kitchen, cooking tools, and ingredients. There should always be adult supervision when use of a sharp tool, oven, or stove is required. Be aware of the symbols below that indicate when special care is necessary.

So, put on your apron and get ready to cheer on your new chef!

SYMBOLS

Hot!
This recipe requires the use of a stove or oven. You will need adult supervision and assistance.

Sharp!
This recipe includes the use of a sharp utensil such as a knife or grater. Ask an adult to help out.

Nuts!
This recipe includes nuts. Find out whether anyone you are serving has a nut allergy.

CONTENTS

NO-BAKE QUICK COOKIES

Who says cookies have to be baked? You can make **amazing** cookies without an oven! No-bake cookies come in many different flavors. They are fun to make anytime.

The no-bake cookie **recipes** in this book are super simple. Cooking teaches you about food, measuring, and following directions. And you get to have **delicious** cookies! Share your tasty creations with family and friends.

COOKING BASICS

Think Safety!

- Ask an adult to help you use a knife. Place things on a cutting board to cut them.

- Clean up spills right away.

- Keep things away from the edge of the table or **counter**.

- Ask an adult to help you use the oven.

- Ask for help if you cannot reach something.

Using the Oven

- Preheat the oven while making the **recipe**.

- Use oven-safe dishes.

- Use pot holders or oven mitts to hold hot things.

- Do not touch the oven door. It can be very hot.

- Set a timer. Check the food and bake longer if needed.

Before Baking

- Get **permission** from an adult.

- Wash your hands.

- Read the recipe at least once.

- Set out the ingredients and tools you will need.

- Keep a **towel** close by for cleaning up spills.

When You're Done

- Let the cookies cool completely.

- Store the cookies in **containers**. Put a sheet of waxed paper in between the **layers** of cookies.

- Put all the ingredients and tools away.

- Wash all the dishes and **utensils**. Clean up your work space.

MEASURING INGREDIENTS

Wet Ingredients

Set a measuring cup on the **counter**. Add the liquid. Stop when it reaches the amount you need. Check the measurement from eye level.

Dry Ingredients

Dip the measuring cup or spoon into the dry ingredient. Fill it with a little more than you need. Use the back of a dinner knife to remove the extra.

Moist Ingredients

Measure ingredients such as brown sugar and dried fruit differently. Press them down into the measuring cup.

DID YOU KNOW THIS = THAT?

There are different ways to measure the same amount.

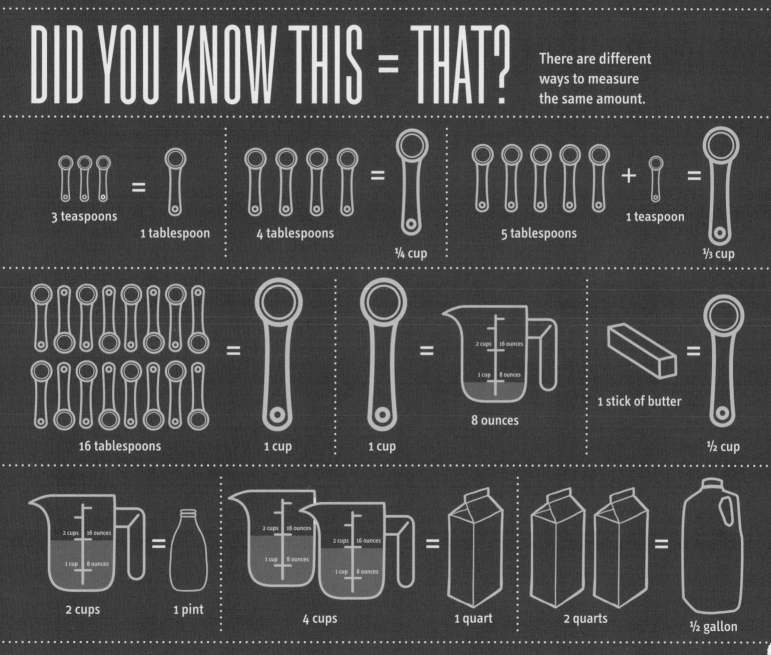

3 teaspoons = 1 tablespoon

4 tablespoons = ¼ cup

5 tablespoons + 1 teaspoon = ⅓ cup

16 tablespoons = 1 cup

1 cup = 8 ounces

1 stick of butter = ½ cup

2 cups = 1 pint

4 cups = 1 quart

2 quarts = ½ gallon

COOKING TERMS

CRUSH

Crush means to mash something into very small pieces.

MELT

Melt means to heat something until it is soft or liquid.

STIR

Stir means to mix ingredients together, usually with a spoon or rubber spatula.

DRIZZLE

Drizzle means to slowly pour a liquid over something.

KITCHEN UTENSILS

lollipop sticks

toothpicks

measuring spoons

measuring cups

medium saucepan

baking sheet

pot holders

mini-muffin tin

plastic zipper bags

electric mixer

microwave-safe bowl

waxed paper

parchment paper

spatula

blender

rolling pin

mixing spoon

mixing bowls

sharp knife

rubber spatula

8 × 8-inch baking dish

aluminum foil

candy thermometer

INGREDIENTS

brown sugar

butter

canola oil

chow mein noodles

corn syrup

cream cheese

creamy peanut butter

crunchy peanut butter

gingersnaps

graham crackers

ground cinnamon

honey

jam

miniature marshmallows

molasses

non-stick cooking spray

oat cereal

Oreos

powdered sugar

raisins

salt

salted peanuts

semi-sweet chocolate chips

vanilla extract

vanilla wafers

white chocolate chips

white sugar

toasty oaty orbs

MAKES 24 COOKIES

INGREDIENTS

1 cup white sugar

1 cup corn syrup

1 cup crunchy peanut butter

6 cups oat cereal

2 teaspoons ground cinnamon

⅓ cup raisins

TOOLS

baking sheet

parchment paper

measuring cups

measuring spoons

medium saucepan

mixing spoon

pot holders

1. Cover the baking sheet with parchment paper.

2. Put the sugar and syrup in a saucepan. Bring it to a boil. Stir **occasionally**. Remove the pan from the heat.

3. Add the remaining ingredients. Stir well.

4. Roll 2 tablespoons of the mixture into a ball. Put the ball on the baking sheet. Repeat until all the mixture is rolled into balls.

sweet
cookie
pops

MAKES 35 COOKIES

INGREDIENTS

1 package Oreos

1 8-ounce package cream cheese

1 cup white chocolate chips

2 tablespoons canola oil

1 cup semi-sweet chocolate chips

. . . .

TOOLS

baking sheet

waxed paper

plastic zipper bag

rolling pin

mixing bowl

electric mixer

sharp knife

lollipop sticks

measuring cups

measuring spoons

microwave-safe bowls

1 Cover the baking sheet with waxed paper.

2 Put some Oreos in a plastic bag. Use a rolling pin to crush the cookies. Put the **crumbs** in a large bowl. Repeat until all of the Oreos are crushed.

3 Add the cream cheese to the crushed Oreos. Mix with an electric mixer.

4 Put the dough on the baking sheet. Press it into a rectangle. Make it about 1 inch (2.5 cm) thick.

19

5 Put waxed paper on top of the dough. Roll over it lightly until the top is smooth. Refrigerate for 10 minutes.

6 Remove the waxed paper. Cut the dough into 1-inch (2.5 cm) squares.

7 Stick a lollipop stick into each square.

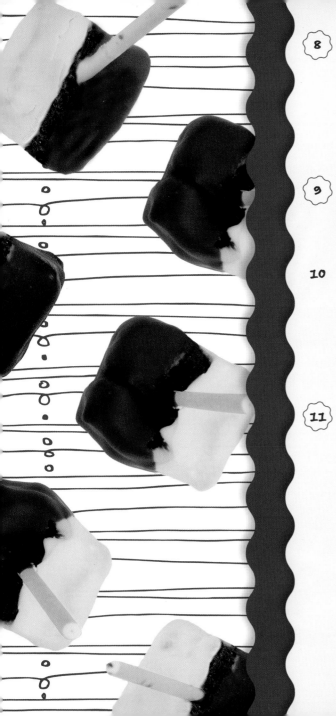

8 Put the white chocolate chips and 1 tablespoon canola oil in a microwave-safe bowl. Microwave on high for 30 seconds. Take it out and stir it. Repeat heating and stirring until the chips are melted.

9 Dip half of each cookie in the white chocolate. Place the cookies on the baking sheet. Let them dry.

10 Put the semi-sweet chocolate chips and 1 tablespoon canola oil in a microwave-safe bowl. Microwave on high for 30 seconds. Take it out and stir it. Repeat heating and stirring until the chips are melted.

11 Dip the other half of each cookie in the chocolate. Place them back on the baking sheet. Let them dry.

delish
cookie
drizzles

INGREDIENTS

1 package gingersnaps

½ cup peanut butter

½ cup brown sugar

1 teaspoon ground cinnamon

1 teaspoon vanilla extract

2 tablespoons molasses

¼ cup white chocolate chips

. . . .

TOOLS

baking sheet

waxed paper

plastic zipper bag

rolling pin

measuring cups

measuring spoons

mixing bowl

mixing spoon

microwave-safe bowl

spoon

1 Cover the baking sheet with waxed paper.

2 Put some gingersnaps in a plastic bag. Use a rolling pin to crush the cookies. Put the **crumbs** in a measuring cup. Repeat until you have 1 cup of crumbs.

3 Put the crushed gingersnaps, peanut butter, sugar, cinnamon, vanilla, and molasses in a mixing bowl. Stir well.

4 Roll the dough into 1-inch (2.5 cm) balls. Place them on the baking sheet.

5 Put the white chocolate chips in a microwave-safe bowl. Microwave on high for 30 seconds. Take it out and stir it. Repeat heating and stirring until the chips are melted.

6 Drizzle the melted chocolate on the cookies. Let them cool.

noodle
stack-ups

INGReDIenTS

1 cup semi-sweet
  chocolate chips
½ cup peanut butter
2 cups chow mein
  noodles
½ cup salted peanuts
½ cup miniature
  marshmallows

. . . .

TOOLS

baking sheet
waxed paper
microwave-safe bowl
spoon
measuring cups

1 Cover the baking sheet with waxed paper.

2 Put the semi-sweet chocolate chips in a microwave-safe bowl. Microwave on high for 30 seconds. Take it out and stir it. Repeat heating and stirring until the chips are melted.

3 Stir in the peanut butter. Add the noodles, peanuts, and marshmallows. Stir gently.

4 Put a spoonful of the mixture on the baking sheet. Press on it with the back of the spoon. Repeat with the rest of the mixture.

5 Refrigerate for 20 minutes.

little chocolate dippers

INGREDIENTS

2 cups peanut butter
3¾ cups powdered sugar
1 teaspoon vanilla extract
14 tablespoons butter
2 cups semi-sweet chocolate
   chips

TOOLS

baking sheet
waxed paper
measuring cups
measuring spoons
mixing bowl
microwave-safe bowl
toothpicks

1   Cover the baking sheet with
    waxed paper.

2   Put the peanut butter, powdered
    sugar, vanilla, and 12 tablespoons
    butter in a large bowl. Stir well.

3   Roll the mixture into 1-inch (2.5 cm)
    balls. Put the balls on the baking
    sheet. Stick a toothpick in each one.
    Refrigerate for 20 minutes.

4   Put the semi-sweet chocolate
    chips and 2 tablespoons butter in a
    microwave-safe bowl. Microwave on
    high for 30 seconds. Take it out and
    stir it. Repeat heating and stirring
    until the chips are melted.

5   Dip the balls in the chocolate. Place
    them back on the baking sheet.
    Refrigerate for 2 hours.

yummy
s'more
bites

INGReDIents

12 graham cracker squares

9 tablespoons butter, melted

non-stick cooking spray

¼ teaspoon salt

¾ cup semi-sweet chocolate chips

1 package miniature marshmallows

½ teaspoon vanilla extract

· · · · · · · · · · · · · · · · · ·

TOOLS

plastic zipper bag

rolling pin

mixing bowl

measuring cups

measuring spoons

mixing spoon

mini-muffin tin

microwave-safe bowl

1   Put the graham crackers in a plastic bag. Use a rolling pin to crush the crackers. Put the **crumbs** in a medium bowl. Stir in 5 tablespoons of melted butter.

2   **Grease** the muffin cups with non-stick cooking spray. Put 1 tablespoon of the graham cracker mixture in each cup. Press it to the bottoms and sides of the cups.

3   Put the salt, remaining butter, ½ cup semi-sweet chocolate chips, and 3 cups marshmallows in a microwave-safe bowl. Microwave on high for 30 seconds. Take it out and stir it. Repeat heating and stirring until the mixture is melted.

4   Add the vanilla and remaining crushed graham crackers. Stir well. Put a tablespoon of the mixture in each muffin cup.

5   Put a marshmallow on each cookie. Put two chocolate chips on each cookie. Freeze for 2 hours.

crunchy pb&j sammies

INGREDIENTS

1 package vanilla wafers
1¼ cups peanut butter
¾ cup honey
1 cup jam

. . . .

TOOLS

baking sheet
waxed paper
plastic zipper bag
rolling pin
measuring cups
mixing bowl
rubber spatula
spoon

1. Cover the baking sheet with waxed paper.

2. Put some vanilla wafers in a plastic bag. Use a rolling pin to crush the cookies. Put the **crumbs** in a measuring cup. Repeat until you have 2 cups of crumbs.

3. Put the crushed cookies, peanut butter, and honey in a mixing bowl. Stir well.

4. Roll the dough into 1-inch (2.5 cm) balls. Place the balls on the baking sheet. Flatten the balls with a spoon. Refrigerate for 2 hours.

5. Put a spoonful of jam on a cookie. Set another cookie on top. Repeat with the rest of the cookies.

GLOSSARY

amazing – wonderful or surprising.

container – something that other things can be put into.

counter – a level surface where food is made.

crumb – a tiny piece of something, especially food.

delicious – very pleasing to taste or smell.

grease – to coat something with butter, oil, or cooking spray.

layer – one thickness of something that may be over or under another thickness.

occasionally – every once in a while.

permission – when a person in charge says it is okay to do something.

recipe – instructions for making something.

towel – a cloth or paper used for cleaning or drying.

utensil – a tool used to prepare or eat food.